Western Poetry
With a Cowboy Flair

Western Poetry
With a Cowboy Flair

Kristine & Family

" Take Care Along the Trail "

Denny Bertrand

7/29/14

Denny Bertrand

Copyright © 2010 by Denny Bertrand.

ISBN: Softcover   978-1-4415-9504-1

All rights reserved. No part of this book may be reproduced or transmitted in any form or by any means, electronic or mechanical, including photocopying, recording, or by any information storage and retrieval system, without permission in writing from the copyright owner.

This book was printed in the United States of America.

To order additional copies of this book, contact:
Xlibris Corporation
1-888-795-4274
www.Xlibris.com
Orders@Xlibris.com
68909

CONTENTS

Forward..9
Acknowledgements..11

The Eagle...12
"The Eagle"...13
Family..14
The Old Brand Inspector...16
"The Old Brand Inspector"...17
My Mom Faye..18
"My Mom Faye"...19
My Daughters..20
"My Daughters"...21
My Uncle Jim...22
"My Uncle Jim"..23
Adrian the Cowboy..24
"Adrian the Cowboy"...25
Friends..26
"Passing of a friend"..28
"Passing of a Friend"...29
Waiting on Zane...32
"Waiting on Zane"..33
Bruce...34
"Bruce"...35
Old Friends..36
"Old Friends"...37
Doc Joe and Me...38
"Doc Joe and Me"...39
Tribute to Maggie..40
"Tribute to Maggie"...41
Waiting on Tex...42
"Waiting on Tex"..43

Zane, Crew and Camper 44
"Zane, Crew and Camper" 45
Big Jim 48
"Big Jim" 49
Memories 50
"Memories" 51
Zwicker 52
"Zwicker" 53
Ranching 54
"Passing of the Cowboy" 56
"Passing of a Cowboy" 57
Cow Camp in the fall 60
"Cow Camp in the fall" 61
Memories of a Cowboy 64
"Memories of a Cowboy" 65
The Cowboy Mom's Nightmare 66
"The Cowboy Mom's Nightmare" 67
Spring Branding 68
"Spring Branding" 69
The Kid and Granddad 70
"The Kid and Granddad" 71
The Old Ranchers Philosophy 72
"The Old Ranchers Philosophy" 73
Then and Now 74
"Then and Now" 75
Does East Meet West 78
"Does East Meet West" 79
Desert Rancher 80
"Desert Rancher" 81
The Ranchers Changes 82
"The Ranchers Changes" 83
Cattleman's Nightmare 84
"Cattleman's Nightmare" 85
Where's the Ranches 86
"Where's the Ranches" 87
The Auctioneer 88
"The Auctioneer" 89
Drought 90
"Drought" 91

Live Stock Auctions..92
The Old Sale Barn...94
"The Old Sale Barn"...95
The Sale Barn Ghost 96
"The Sale Barn Ghost"...97
My Market Philosophy...98
"My Market Philosophy"...99
The Sorter 100
"The Sorter"..101
Cattle Buyer 102
"Cattle Buyer"...103
Bad Day for the Boss...104
"Bad Day for the Boss"...105
The Trader 106
"The Trader"...107
The Gambler...108
"The Gambler" 109
Rodeo 110
Cowboy Reunion 112
"Cowboy Reunion"...113
Mr. Rodeo...114
"Mr. Rodeo"...115
Rodeo Time 116
"Rodeo Time" 117
Mr. Bronc Man 118
"Mr. Bronc Man" 119
Out of Chew...120
"Out of Chew"...121
Stranger 122
"Stranger"...123
The Coffee Shop Cowboy's 124
"The Coffee Shop Cowboys"...125
Rodeo Cowboys and Gates..126
"Rodeo Cowboy's and Gates"...127
When a Legend Fades..128
"When a Legend Fades" 129
Windmills 130
"Wind Mills"...131
"Nature"..133

Weather Changes 134
"Weather Changes" 135
No Rain 136
"No Rain" 137
"My Horses" 139
The Trainer 140
"The Trainer" 141
The Last of the Wild Ones 142
"The Last of the Wild Ones" 143
"The Renegade Mules" 145
Yard Sale Queens..146
"Yard Sale Queens" 147
"American Farmer" 149
The Local Politician 150
"The Local Politician" 151
Make It Beef...152
"Make It Beef" 153
The Week before Christmas 154
"The Week before Christmas" 155
"Christmas Eve" 157
New Years Eve 160
"New Years Eve" 161
"Christmas"..165
"Christmas Alone"..167
Angels of Love..168
"Angles of Love" 169

Forward

I'm going to start out this book with probably my favorite poem *"The Eagle"* I wrote this poem on January 31, 2001. In 2002 and 2003 the poem had received an Honorable Mention both years from the Famous Poetry Society. From there I am breaking this down into categories for how they pertain. I hope that the friends I've written about don't get upset because my words are true. I write as I see things, some funny, some serious, but, I couldn't write these if it wasn't for all of you.

Thank you to a bunch a friends that I have been truly blessed with.

Take Care

Denny

Acknowledgements

I want to thank my family. My parents Faye and Benton Bertrand. My first poem started with the Old Brand Inspector. I will not lie to you but to this day I cannot sit down and write a poem just to make one, some event or happening will bring the words to me.

My brother Jim and sister Sandy Story, my daughters Billie Jo, Dusti and Codi. But these poems would not have happened if not for the eventst of all the friends I have written about.

Thank you for all being there and bringing the inspirations to me. I want to give a special thanks to my cousin Dolores Sheets for getting this ready for publishing. A big thanks to Renn and Ross for giving me a chance to make this happen at Xlibris publishing.

With heartfelt thanks to all of you

Denny

The Eagle

I wrote this poem about when I was living on Dr. M.J. Nachtriebs Ranch at Northrop, Colorado.

In the mornings as I would leave to work I would see this pair of eagles above in their nest in a tree. At night when I got home I wouldn't see them, but just before dark they would fly over the camper I was staying in.

I always liked to think they were watching over me.

"The Eagle"

High in the tree tops
He sits all alone
Looking out across the valley
That he claims as home

I have sat and watched him
As he soars in the sky
He floats real graceful
And I wonder why

He is an American symbol
For freedom in our land
He is peaceful and proud
But if needed he'll make a stand

The great American eagle
I hope like us, he remains free
He makes a stand for Independence

As he watches over you and me

Family

After starting out this book with ***The Eagle***, with all the pressing issues we have now, the most important thing we have is family. Even I have not written a lot of poems in this category. Doesn't mean I don't think of them, for some odd reason, I can't make up a poem. It just takes something to bring the words to me. I don't understand this, some tell me it is inspiration.

The Old Brand Inspector

I wrote this poem originally about my dad **Benton T. Bertrand** who was a Colorado State Brand Inspector for over 30 years. He not only knew all of the state livestock laws, but also any brands in his district, their owners and type of livestock they ran. Dad had a photographic memory, once he saw the brand he could remember who they were and where they were from. It kind of makes me sad with the inspectors we have now, too many of them can't remember anyone's brand much less find it on a cow.

Dad this is not only for you, but to the Brand Inspectors that make things right. I want to mention a few: Don Crain, Earl Brown, Ed Paul, Tom Moss, Dewey Boyd, Errol Raley, Earl Haller, Jack Hall, Les Davis, Bob Dilley, Gene Pepogle, Walter Scott, Paul Scott, Don Pursley, and Ed Humphrie. These are just a few I remember, they took their jobs serious, donated a lot of personal time. They were always there for the livestock owner.

October 1996

"The Old Brand Inspector"

He walks out of his office
With clippers and rope in hand
He can hardly drive his pickup
But he damn sure can read a brand

From Johnny's trading pens
To the sale barn til night
He looks at cows and horses
And has the owner's right

But to you and I, who laugh with glee
About the brands he calls out;
Until he clips the hair for us to see
We are shocked with no doubt

My hats off to him
A friend we all know
To the brand inspector
From a long time ago

My Mom Faye

I wrote this about my mom **Faye Bertrand**, she was very active in the Colorado Cattle Women's Association (Cowbells) for almost 30 years.
She received the award of *Cattle Women of the Year* in the fall of 1998. But due to my dad's failing health, she didn't get her award until June of 1999. Dad made sure all of the family were there when she received the award at the convention in Crested Butte, Colorado that year. That was probably the highlight of dad's year, Dad passed away two months later in August.

November 27, 1998

"My Mom Faye"

The 1998 State Cattlewomen of the Year
Was not really in her plan
To speak to a crowd she has to hide her fear
But she is a true daughter of the land

From a homestead family in the southwest of the state
She can handle any chore
From fixing hair to building a gate
And was willing to-do more

Her life from Cortez, Denver to Salida and back
She kept her family happy and fed
For enthusiasm she never lacked
From the time she was up, she always sped

From sale barns to ranches and even town
She never met a stranger
Or let a friend down
Even through sickness or danger

But, mom this is from me
When you receive your plaque, remain proud
For whatever is going to be
You have the right to yell loud

My Daughters

I wrote this poem about my three daughters

Billy Jo
Dusty
and
Codi

They are still this way just as in the poem says, and I love them all the same. Between the three of them they have blessed me with six wonderful grandkids that I adore. All three girls were active in school, Billy was in FFA, 4 H and horse shows she also roped and barrel raced in rodeos, Dusty was in sports, rodeo and 4 H with Codi doing the same. There were several years that they were the toughest competition between each other. They have brought home many awards between them. Billy now lives in Salida has a daughter and a son, Dusty and Casey live at Dove Creek have two daughters and one son, Cody and Heath are in Salida and have one daughter and are expecting another this summer I am proud of all three daughters and what they have accomplished.

August 16, 1999

"My Daughters"

Even though I love you all the same
You are all precious and fit your name
Billie you have always been the one that was strong
Even when everyone else was wrong

And then there was little Dusti
You always smooth over anything that is crusty
And I know you can go an extra mile
All it takes is your smile

And there is ornery little Codi
Her little smile reminds you of a coyote
She is precious just the same
But she lives up to her name

I don't love anyone of you the most
But your all my daughter's I'm proud to boast
Just remember me when you smile
It will make me go a long while

I love you all and that's what means the most
I'm proud of you and I will always boast
You are all the best I'm proud to say
You will all succeed in your own way

I love you all and maybe it's too late
But one of your hugs set it straight
But just remember that I'm your Dad
I really didn't want to make you sad

My Uncle Jim

This is a poem I wrote for my Mom's older brother *Jim Wilson* for his memorial service. Jim was a very quiet person, yet at the same time he did many good deeds for friends and the community. He served his country in World War II at the Battle of the Bulge in Normandy. Jim farmed for many years and all of us still think of
him with pride.

"My Uncle Jim"

He was born to a homestead family
In Montezuma County and farming was his
Pride
He worked hard for his family
With wife Veda by his side

He devoted his life to their family
Robert, Terry and Faye
His farm was neat and clean
That was just his way

He was born to Nancy & Charles Wilson
And James Everett was his name
With eleven brothers and sisters
He loved them all the same

He was also a World War II Veteran
And his country was proud of him
I will always say with pride
That he was my Uncle Jim

Adrian the Cowboy

When my uncle Adrian Bradfield passed away, his son Wilson called and asked me to write a poem for his services. I was honored yet, I had a problem, and sometimes my thinker doesn't think so fast. This was probably one of the hardest poems I ever wrote. Because most of my poems just come to me. I thought and wrote, wrote and thought but nothing came to me, in the middle of the night the words came I woke up and wrote them down, thanks to technology I was able to fax them for the services with four hours left to go.

July 27, 2002

"Adrian the Cowboy"

I will always remember his stories
The more he told the faster he would talk
The son of a pioneer ranch family
He was on horseback before he could walk

He never had the silver tappings
Or wore a pair of chinks
The outlaw broncs he rode
Now would be called dinks

The cowboy now days would make fun of him
They haven't had to take care of cattle on the rim
With a bronze and nickel horned saddle
And soft inlaid rope

He would always watch them in the brush
The arena cowboy would have no hope

In his boots, Levi's and old brown hat
He was proud of being a cowboy
He lived and told stories with a grin
All of us knew him as Adrian

Friends

Now this section is my favorite of all, because of the friends and things they have done brought the words to me. I have been fortunate to see their downsides. Yet see them rebound and make the best of things. I hope I haven't caused insult to anyone of them, I just wrote what I have seen. But without my friends and memories I wouldn't be able to write these words today, once again a big *thank you* to all my friends.

2000

"Passing of a friend"

All my life I have been blessed with good Friends
Good horses and dog's but the
Greatest thing that ever happened to me
Was a Border Collie I named Hoagie
For thirteen years we were together
He just knew what we needed to do
He was a great companion and
I could feel his love and trust,
No matter what I did he was always there
Whether
Gathering cattle or loading sheep on a truck
I knew he did care,
He had a way of lookin at me,
With his eye's he said, "It would be alright"
But after all
These years I say, Hoagie where are you tonight

"Passing of a Friend"

When we first met each other
It has been thirteen years past
Through good and hard times
We were friends to the last

He and I worked a lot of cattle
From early morning until night late
We never argued or crossed each other
But going home he always beat me to the gate

His day always started out happy
He worked hard to earn his keep
It didn't matter if it was dry
Or raining and the mud deep

There was something about him
And it was easy to earn my trust
He was a constant companion
And life to him was happy and just

And now he has left and went on
He passes away on March twenty seven
I have just one hope that God
Works Border Collies in heaven
Good bye Hoagie

Waiting on Zane

This last spring Zane's wife Linda and I were waiting on trucks hauling cattle back to Cortez, Colorado from Bluff, Utah.
Linda made a remark and this poem is dedicated to her. All she said was, "Why are we always waiting on Zane."

"Waiting on Zane"

Oh the words I'm writing are so true
It's the truth I'm telling to you
About a friend of mine in the southwest
When it comes to friends he is the best

In business dealing's he is nothing but fair
For other people he does really care
As a cowboy he is one of the best
I'd match him against anyone in the west

Now to me his is nothing but a great friend
I would defend him to the bitter end
His ways are honest and very true
He wouldn't do anything to hurt me or you

Now to do thing's with him day to day
He get's to visiting that's just his way
Sometimes I think he can't tell time
But hearing his stories suits me fine

Dang, if I ain't in a hurry to get home
But now he's busy again on the phone
I'm not mad or one to complain
But once again I'm waiting on Zanc

Bruce

I could fill pages about Bruce Gum, what all he did for me and others. But I could not tell you everything and how he helped so many. I will just let it go as the best friend and boss anyone could know.

November 13, 1998

"Bruce"

The man I work for is not only
A boss, but a friend
He's one to ride the river with
And stick with you to the end

It doesn't matter what time of day
How tough or bad the conditions are
He'll make you laugh in some way
It's just his nature to do so

He's a good judge of cattle or man
He might joke and mess around
But he always sticks with his plan
Honesty and fairness are his way

If you brag to his family
You might get told
After they made Bruce Gum
They threw away the mold

Old Friends

After all these years of writing this I still get choked up when I read it. An old friend of our family Edker Wilson of Lajara, Colorado and I were talking on the phone one day. Edker was a rodeo producer in the four state area of New Mexico, Arizona, Colorado and Utah. He helped many young cowboys' get started rodeoing. Some of them moved on and became World Champions. I had told Edker that all the years I had announced Rodeo's I regretted I had never announced one for him, Edker just replied with, "Denny I know that, but you were always a friend."
This was inspired by an old family friend and my mentor Edker Wilson.

April 16, 2002

"Old Friends"

I was talking on the phone
To an old friend the other day
When he spoke his wisdom
It just came my way

He said, son life can be hard
And a lot of things seem in just
You won't make it though
Without a friend you can trust

Now awards I've had many
And material things more than a few
But if it wasn't for old friends
I would have never made it through

Through good times and hard ones
Just remember when things aren't right
That you're never really alone
You're friends are with you day and night

If you don't believe what I say
And you still have a lot of doubt
Just always try to remember
Friends in life are what it's all about

Doc Joe and Me

After all the year's that have gone by since Doc Joe passed away. I still have precious memories of Doctor M.J. Nachtrieb DVM, his wife Viola and son's Joe Dave, Chris and Dan. I still keep in contract with the boys, we will always be friends. I think back on the years in school that I was with Doc Joe as much as with my own family. Joe was one of the bet vets I have ever known. He had always preferred working on large animals. He was the son of a pioneer family that were the first to settle at Nathrop. Joe was also the vet at the Salida Sale Barn for years, but being allergic to antibiotics he basically had to retire from his practice and was a meat inspector until he retired. He continued to run the ranch at Nathrop, Colorado until he passed away. To this day I often think of him and miss his crooked grin.

"Doc Joe and Me"

It has taken a lot of years
Cause of memories don't you see
But it feels good to write
About times past with Doc Joe and me

He was known across the state
As a veteranian he was one of the best
But he was stubborn and independent
And a client's nerve he would test

Being a son of a pioneer rancher
At Northrop in the county of Chaffee
He was always there to help
Animal lover's like you and me

From farms, ranches and a sale barn
He showed up with his crooked grin
Always laughing and teasing with a smile
There was no way but to love him

Now the years have passed by
And my memories have never faded
I will always love and respect Joe
But he tagged a name on me I hated

Joe always called me to help on calls
He would start the day with toast and jelly
Then he would always grin and say
Are you ready to work dough belly

Tribute to Maggie

About three years ago I was watching Midwest Country being broadcast from Sandstone Minn. When this young lady started singing. I just had to have her CD. I contacted the theatre and they gave me her address and phone number. Maggie Mae, her husband Roger and myself have kept in contact with each other through the years and have became great friends. If you want to hear her sing or want a CD just contact Maggie Mae's Café in Oxford, Wisconsin.

(P.S. you owe me a cup of coffee Maggie and Roger)

Keep up the good work.

September 18, 1998

"Tribute to Maggie"

Now the lady I'm writing about
I hope all of you can understand
That her dream to be a known singer
Will happen for her across this big land

Now when it comes to singing
She honestly sings from her heart
Teaching herself to yodel, and play guitar
That was just her beginning and start

Actually I don't know much
But I am a truly dedicated fan
With her determination and Roger's help
I hope she's famous across the land

She and her husband farm in Wisconsin
They raise a crop of soybeans and corn
They work hard together with their family
And always start in the early morn

If you want to start out very happy
In Oxford Wisconsin you can start your day
For breakfast and to hear her sing
Just go to Maggie Mae's country café

Waiting on Tex

This poem is for a very good friend of mine Tex Vaughn of Stratford, Texas.
Yes, everybody at any sale barn waits on Tex.

November 9, 1998

"Waiting on Tex"

We had another sale today
It was snowing, blowing and raining
And miserable in every possible way
But the sale is now over

It has been over for hours now
We have most of the buyers yard backs done
All the crew is in the office
Just waiting for our usual one

I think maybe something's wrong
I've been cursed with a hex
Cause once again it happened
We're still waiting on Tex

Zane, Crew and Camper

We were sitting at the Sale Barn Café at Cow House Auction in
Kirtland, New Mexico. When my good friend Zane Odell was telling this
story. They were staying in this old round top single axel camper trailer and
they hadn't put blocks under it to stabilize it. Ray Hatch, Shane Hatch, Phil
Wiseman, Jim Bramwell and myself couldn't stop laughing yet the way Zane
told it you knew it had to be true. I wrote this poem that night because I
thought it was a story that needed to be told,
Thanks Zane

June 2, 2008

"Zane, Crew and Camper"

Now this story I want to tell
Is not made up but really true
When Zane told the story
I laughed and turned blue

They were out gathering cattle
In the brush, cedars and pines
They had passed a jug around
And they all felt very fine

Cause they knew Zane for supper
Would fix good chile and beans
They would sleep full and happy
And contented by all means

Now Zane cooked their supper
It was really chile and beans
He passed two bowls of chile out
And things went to hell it seems

When the boy's shifted back
That is when things went to hell
The camper stood on it's end
All they could do was yell

When all this was happening
Zane heard nothing but the dog's yelp
He was really concerned
But he didn't know how to help

Its seems the dog's were in trouble
And Zane never really thought
The dogs were at the end of the camper
Just doing what they were taught

When everything settled down
And they crawled out the door
When they got on the ground
Zane's chile they wanted no more

Zane just looked up and frowned
As they brought the camper
Back on its wheels and the ground
He knew everything was right

So he just turned the dogs in
To eat the chile and beans
He knew everybody was happy
And contented by all means

Big Jim

I don't really know if the words to this Poem I wrote about Jim Suckla will
do honor to him. Jim built a legacy through the years.
This past August the sale barn here at Cortez, the Cortez
Livestock Auction celebrated their 50th year. Judd and Rowdy have turned
the sale barn over to their grandson's to manage.
They continue the tradition of ranching and running the sale barn.
But you know that, my hats off to Big Jim

April 10, 2002

"Big Jim"

To those of us that knew him
In the southwest arid land
He put together many holdings
And was proud of the cattle with his brand

The Suckla name was known and respected
But to us that really knew him
From announcing rodeos, auctioneering or running a sale
We all knew him as Big Jim

Helen and Jim started out with nothing
And build a sale barn on the family farm
He had a natural way of doing things
And making things work was a charm

Jim was never afraid to get up and work
He was on the go and thinking all day
He never had time to slow down
Nobody ever knew, that was just his way

And to his family I am proud to say
I have been inspired many times by him
He had a nickname many didn't know
I'll tell you out of respect it was Diamond Jim

Memories

This is about some old family friends that were in the live stock business together for many years. It seemed like when Bent died one by one they all just followed. This group of friends is loved and missed by many in Colorado and New Mexico

Dedicated to the memory of
Benton Bertrand
Buddy Waggoner
Jim Suckla
Doug Frazier
and
Dwight Wallace

April 29, 2002

"Memories"

Memories are really hard to live with
They come to you almost everyday
In your mind you think of something else
But your loved one's memories are there to stay

It started out almost three years ago
With my Dad, then Buddy, Big Jim, Doug then Dwight
We thought they would live forever
It seemed they left us overnight

The good Lord said he needed them
He had too many cow traders in Heaven
He needed two Auctioneers, two Brand Inspectors
And one Rancher
Just to make the odds ten to seven

During everyday they worked hard
To make a living just to survive
They wouldn't have made it without
Faye, Carolyn, Helen, Paula, or Jackie their wives

Somewhere in Heaven they are gathered
Around some sale barn with each other
They weren't only good friends and partners
But treated each one as a brother

Zwicker

I basically wrote this poem about Eldon Zwicker who was one of my dad's best friends. Eldon was not only a good rancher, a great cowboy, but a real true friend. He accomplished many things as a rancher. But to take credit for anything he remained humble to the very end.

June 10, 2000

"Zwicker"

He was affectionately know as Zwick
Across the vast Four Corners land
He wasn't only a good cowboy
But as a rancher he was a top hand

From the hills of the state capital
He could visit with the politician or the social elite
To the broken down man
That he just met on the street

In the spring his family and cattle
To the Beaver Mountain country they'd go
Until they started the fall gather
To get out of the mountains before the winter snow

Down in McElmo Canyon with his wife Lila
They raised their family with pride
They taught each one the values of life
Along with caring for cattle and how to ride

In the Cattleman's Association
He was respected and well known
He always enjoyed his friends at meetings
But was also glad to get home

Whether at the ranch or cow camp
At his home or in front of a camp fire flicker
He was honest and contended
This man Eldon Zwicker

Ranching

I don't think anyone knows or can predict where the future of ranching is headed for or the changes we will see. I know as long as people need to eat the farmers and ranchers will do the best they can to survive. They make sure we will all be able to eat from the past to present and future. It is up to all of us to give them the respect and the credit they so much deserve. Because without them we would not be able to live, you can live on vegetables, chicken, fish pork and beef. But try to eat your computer and survive.

October 18, 1999

"Passing of the Cowboy"

I probably wrote this poem out of spite
I remember the day's when I rode for
Eleven Mile Grazing Assoc. at Hartsel, CO

To the day's I rode pens in the feed lots at
Kearney County Feeders, Lakin, KS
Burlington Commercial Feeders at Burlington, CO
and Ox Town Cattle Feeders at Tribune, KS after
I moved back there, where was home

What a shock to me.
I was at the store and post office
When a pickup and stock trailer
Pulled up next to me

The two men got out of their pickup
Wearing spurs and chaps.
They went in and ordered cappuccino
Sayin they could of gathered all the cattle

If they hadn't run out of gas
You'll
Probably guess that in the trailer they had
A motorcycle and a four wheeler

"Passing of a Cowboy"

I was in town the other day
When this pickup and trailer came my way
In the front of the trailer there was a steer
And taking up the back was a four wheeler

I went to the store to get a new hat
And maybe some jeans with this and that
The hats were gone replaced by caps
On the back wall were coveralls instead of chaps

I went to the end of the store with hope
All the tack was gone there wasn't even a rope
I asked the store keeper why the change
He said son the cows are all from the range

Horses and cowboys are no longer needed
They've lost their forest and BLM and barely have their deeded
The people here now live the city way
They don't think about beef these days

What's gonna happen when the ranchers are gone
Will we just see them in movies and in song
But it shore hurts my feelings these days
Just to see the passing of the cowboy ways

Cow Camp in the fall

This poem was from memories as I was in my teens. I helped Glenn and Jerry Everett gather cattle at their cow camp north of Salida, Colorado. We were riding as hard as we could when it started to snow, in two days the snow was deep and we got the cattle home, Glenn paid me and said, "You coming back next year?" Guess what I did, I feel very blessed not only knowing Glenn and Terry their wives Jeannie and Judy, but also their mom Wilmoth, and their dad George Jr. and what a giant of a man their granddad George looked to me, on his buckskin horse starched shirt and tie his memory will never fade. I don't know why.

This is dedicated *to Terry and Glenn Everett* of Salida, Colorado

October 4, 1999

"Cow Camp in the fall"

There is nothing like the mountains
When you're gathering cattle in the fall
And colors of the aspen leaves turning
And the lonely bull elks bugle call

You spend many days in the saddle
The cows and calves are fat and sleek
But as you ride along you're always looking
To see if snow is coming on the highest peak

You gather cattle off the high points
And ride every valley and down every draw
But riding along you day dream
About the different wildlife you saw

You think about all the riding
And the lonely night's at cow camp
How next year you'll do something different
But you better hurry because it's getting damp

When you get the cattle moved down home
And head to town for a day or so
You can't wait for the spring thaw
Cause back to cow camp you get to go

Memories of a Cowboy

What really inspired me when I wrote this poem, was remembering
The old cowboys and ranchers that I grew up around. They were the old
cowboys that worked day and nite. They rode any horse they could, knowing
when they got home they had put in a good day. They weren't afraid of any
horse or scared to rope a cow. No matter what they got the job done. The
country was rough, not in an arena where practice makes perfect. In the
rough country every loop counts, it doesn't matter if your horse is buckin
you have to get the job done

June 19, 2009

"Memories of a Cowboy"

Tonight we are at the chuck wagon
But today we gathered round
With our heads bowed and hat's off
We laid another cowboy in the ground

There wasn't a horse he was afraid of
And he was bucked off very few
He wasn't really a bronc rider
He just knew what to do

And for all the ranches
Across the great ole land
He was a true cowboy at heart
He always rode for the brand

I know the life of a cowboy
Is almost a way of the past
With all the changes in ranch in
I pray his memory does last
And Lord I pray in so many ways
At the pearly gates. He won't wait in line
Give him broncs to ride and cattle to rope
That will suit him just fine

The Cowboy Mom's Nightmare

Now, I'm going to throw a kink into things. Most songs are written from poems. But this poem came to me from a song the "Cattle Call" as I said earlier. It just takes something to get my pea brain workin and the words just come. So I want to say that I've bought used up my older friends so I have to pick on kids now. I want to dedicate this poem to Bronco Odell and his sister Cailey. They are two very polite and great kids to be around, yet both of them know the cowgirl and cowboy way.

"The Cowboy Mom's Nightmare"

The coyotes are a howling
The Cowboys are a squalling
Cause they got to get up early morn
Our of their bedrolls so warm

But when the sun peeks over the mountain
Their fears are soon forgotten
Because they know across this big land
They are honest and ride for the brand

As they saddle their broncs in the rising sun
They know he's going to buck, the sun of a gun
So in the saddle he screws himself down tight
But buckin to the left, he bucks off the right

Now in his head the bells are ringing
He hears his momma's voice a singing
My son always had broncs, but not a toy
Why did we let him be a cowboy

But she smiles and says with pride
He's a cowboy and knows how to ride
He will ride hard to the end of the day
Cause he grew up knowin the cowboy way

Spring Branding

I wrote this poem when I was in Guymon OK and was in the Borger, Texas arena. I stopped by the legendary Four Sixes Ranch (6666) at Panhandle Texas. Their trailers, horses, cowboy's, cowgirl's, wives and kids were everywhere, they had gathered and branded 600 calves that day. Oh how the memories hit me when I was a kid in Chaffee County in Colorado. When for two months on week ends we would help neighbors brand. I will always remember the meals fed to us at day's end. Guess what, I got asked to stay for dinner at the 6666's that day.
I hope this tradition doesn't go away.

December 24, 1998

To all the cowgirls, cowboys and youngsters across this great nation.

"Spring Branding"

It begins during the year
When the birds start to sing
It's the ranch ritual
The yearly spring branding

Whether there are a lot of neighbors
Of there are just a few
From cowhands, wives and old timers
To the single hands, or the little buckaroo

On each of the ranches they gather
The cattle across the land
Until everyone's calves are worked
And carry each rancher's brand

But now days ranching is different
Than when you could prove up on the land
The ranchers are mortgaged to the hilt
Just to have a financial plan

But the way things are going
The land they may have to sell
For the spring branding may become a story
For us when we are old timers

The Kid and Granddad

This poem goes back to a family at Salida, Colorado when Grandpa George Everett was telling me about when his family settled in Chaffee County. Though many years have passed, I will always remember George, he was a gentleman, but till he passed away nobody really knew what he had done. I was maybe eight or nine years old when we were gathering cattle on Sand Park. The horse I was riding jumped from a rattlesnake, course I wasn't the best at handling a horse yet. I landed on my head and knees in the sand I really thought I'd bawl. I'll remember the words Grandpa George said to me I don't know why. He looked and said,
"Button Cowboys don't cry."

May 29, 1999

"The Kid and Granddad"

The kid and the old-timer
Saddled up and headed west
The kid just followed along
Because the old cowboy knew best
They headed out on a steady trout
Away from their cozy camp
They set a pace that was fast
It was cold and the weather damp
The kid loved the stories as they went along
The old man told without fail
About how things were tough and hard
On the old Loving Goodnight Trail
His granddad would tell about the land
As they searched and hunted for the cows
When it had not been disturbed
By the big tractors and wide plows
The kid knows that his futures not the best
Even though he love's his granddad through
His is now living in a new and troubled west
Ranching has changed, but what can he do
It doesn't really matter that he cared
About the open range that is gone at last
He lives for his granddads daily stories
And is proud of his granddad's past

The Old Ranchers Philosophy

This is for all the old hands that made it through tough times. Some of us will always remember you. This poem goes back to all of the old ranchers I've known. The list would be way too long to write about. I am so grateful that I had the pleasure to know some of these gentlemen, their wives and families, when ranching was a way of life and not about money.

January 06, 1999

"The Old Ranchers Philosophy"

I was talking to an old rancher
While we were sitting under a pine
Visiting about how things were
When he started talking about old times

He told about life when ranches
All joined and ran on open ranges
About roundups behind a chuck wagon
Being able to live on a pocketful of change

And how it was to work for an outfit
Under the management of one man
To know all the time what was happening
And not to follow a computer plan

He was glad about the life he had led
His time was about over without a doubt
And said the ranches would be gone soon
We would just have cow farms to think about

Then and Now

I wrote this poem in December 1998. It was at the time, how things were, and were changing. It wasn't meant to downgrade a lifestyle or to put anyone down. It was just as life was. And how the people lived day to day.

"Then and Now"

Have you ever been in the Oklahoma Panhandle?
Riding across the country alone
And wondered what it would have been like
To have lived here when there wasn't a phone

To have lived in a shoddy with wood for heat
Or to have to go to the well to get a drink
When you raised a garden and your meat
And everything was stored in a cellar

When most of your clothes were handmade
And neighbors came to visit
When everyone gathered in the shade
And enjoyed each others company

When all travel was horseback
Or with a wagon and team
They didn't have payments
On a fancy computerized machine

To make an honest living
And not depend on a big loan
But to work hard with your family
And have no need to leave your home

When payments and taxes
Were not a controlling factor
And all the farming was done
Without a big ole tractor

So I wonder if times were really that hard
It seems now we live in frustration
With high taxes and government control
And living in a confused nation

So were things really that bad
They didn't have a high mortgage
On everything they owned or had
So are we the ones really living hard

Does East Meet West

Every time I read this poem I get confused. As it says there's
ranches and cowboys across our great nation. I think I'm going
too look again on the map and try to find where the hell does east meet
the west.

February 4, 1999

"Does East Meet West"

I've been across this nation
And I don't like to boast
From north to south
And from coast to coast

But I sometimes wonder
To figure it out I try my best
When it comes to ranching
Where does east meet west?

I know there's a ranch in Texas
Along the river called the Canadian
But there are also ranches
In Pennsylvania's Appalachian's

One of the nations biggest is in Florida
A ranch of several thousand acres "The Deseret"
But there are ranches as big in Idaho
Also in Louisiana where gators are a threat

But when it comes to where ranches are
And you want to try a real test
Just try to figure out on a map
Where does east meet west?

Desert Rancher

If I was to dedicate this poem to anyone, it would be to all the Cowboys and Ranchers struggling to make a living anywhere that they could make it or go broke just depending on the rain. And how the families have stayed together hoping for a better next year.

January 26, 2000

"Desert Rancher"

High on a mesa on his horse alone
Looking down across the wide valley
For sixty some years he's called home
He glances at the cows for a quick tally

He turned and looked to the west
To make a living was hard on this desert land
Working hard everyday he did his best
Dedicating himself and doing all he can

Ranching ain't easy that is true
There are things that go wrong everyday
It will cause an old rancher to think what to do
But time will always tell and he'll make it someway

Being a rancher on the desert will test any man
It takes a lot of acres to run just a cow
Just surviving you do the best you can
In an arid and rocky ground you couldn't plow

But a year with good rain and everything goes right
Weaning calves on a market that is good at last
He can go to bed and rest easy at night
He forgets all the hard years he's had in the past

Through the years his family has been by his side
Helping with the ranch in true dedication
Never worrying about how hard they had to ride
He knows the ranch will carry on for several generations

The Ranchers Changes

I'll be short here and let the poem say it all. This is dedicated to all the ranchers, their families and how they've hung on.

December 17, 1998

"The Ranchers Changes"

I remember back when I was a kid
The rancher was quiet and humble
And proud of everything he did

He sold on an open market across the land
His market was sure and steady
And controlled by supply and demand

He was able to live and buy on what he could afford
He sold at auctions and private treaty
And wasn't controlled by the futures board

His worries only amounted to remain free
To produce cattle and make a living
Now he has to fight the Big Three

He didn't have to fight from day to day
He was not controlled by these groups
The government, the cities and the E.P.A.

Now he really doesn't know what do to
He's just trying to survive
And not be the beef in their stew

Cattleman's Nightmare

This poem relates to where the ranchers and I have to laugh and think about the environmentalist and tree huggers. How at night they go to sleep after having a good meal in there stick built homes, after having a good meat dish whether chicken, beef or fish. They wake up trying to stop ranching, farming, mining or gas & oil production. They never think about what they use or need or the people that produce it. They are just stingy in their thoughts. If all the ranches, farmers, miners and oil field people would shut down then we would see a very pitiful sight and a new way of life.

"Cattleman's Nightmare"

Last night I had a dream about a ride
I saddled at Nathrop and headed out
I went north to Leadville and over the divide
It was on Battle Mountain I figured my route

On down the mountain on an old cattle trail
I really enjoyed the view
Until I ran smack dad into the condos of Aspen and Vail
I noticed then that ranchers were few

I headed to Dillon and Frisco just to see
To my surprise all the ranches were gone
To make room for growth on I-70
So I turned south and headed on

Down to Fairplay and into South Park
To a land turned desert from water being sold
From years before when developers left their mark
The water went to Colorado Springs and Denver so big and bold

I headed on over to Saddle Mountain to Guffey
And on the hillsides were houses in line
To be sold to some city yuppie
I rode out and to Highway Nine

Onto Cotopaxi and Salida
To where, then I wanted to flee
Because where there's a mountain
A cow you won't see

Where's the Ranches

When I wrote this poem in 1996, I had just moved back to Colorado and saw how the land development had cut up all the ranches through central Colorado. What a pity when this goes on.

February 12, 1996

"Where's the Ranches"

I was driving along the other day
When this thought occurred to me
On all this land where houses stand
Were where the ranches used to be

I went out to look at an 80 acre pasture
Where 20 years ago I had got stuck
It is now a protected habitat
For one lonely duck

I went on to an area where there were large meadows
Where ranchers put up tons of hay
Which has now been condemned from ranching
For a place for city people to play

In driving on I went on to the forest service
And walked on an old cattle trail
Where cattle are not allowed to graze
It is protected for deer, elk and quail

I think that it won't be long
When all the farmers and ranchers
Will be remembered only in verse and song
They were forced out of business by people

And when the people are hungry
And the environmentalists need something to do
They can go see what is left of sheep and cattle
Down at their local zoo.

The Auctioneer

This is dedicated to all the auctioneers not only in livestock, but anything they sell. They balance on a tight rope trying to meet a fine line. To keep consigners happy and yet keep the buyers feeling fine.

November 7, 1998

"The Auctioneer"

He sits on the Auction block
With gavel in hand
He'll run a fast sale today
Cause that's his plan

He'll sell anything from furniture
To cattle, sheep and ducks
From horses to implements
To tractors, cars and trucks

He'll start something at a hundred
And run it to one seventy five
It's just his way to see
If the crowd's alive

Auctioneering is his living
And he has made it a game
Of getting sellers the most dollars
It's the way he got in the Auctioneer's Hall of Fame

Drought

One of the most frustrating and hard times can happen from Mother Nature and that is as drought. It can hit anywhere and anytime. And nobody has any control over what happens next.

June 12, 2002

"Drought"

Once again the day starts out early
With a hot blistering sun
The drought covers seven states
And has an effect on everyone

The farm crops are dry and shriveled
Because of no winter snow or rain
From Colorado, Kansas and Oklahoma Panhandle
The farmers all have a look of pain

North to the Rocky Mountain of Colorado
That stand barren because of no snow
To the plains of Colorado and Kansas
The farm ground is starting to blow

All across these great western states
Colorado, Kansas, Oklahoma and New Mexico
The ranchers are sending cattle to sale barns
They have no choice it's the only place to go

Now as I travel across this dry land
They say that paybacks are hell
With everyone living in desperation
Then Mother Nature has done well

Live Stock Auctions

Livestock auctions are better known as sale barns, they have been a big part of my life. I basically was born into this lifestyle and being 57 years old it is still a big part of my life. Though at the present with video auctions, and auctions on the internet, the old sale barns still survive. I think the reason is it still brings the farming and ranching communities together. There will always be a need for the sale barn. The video's and internet sales work great for the bigger operations.
The small operator still needs a place to sell his livestock. The local sale barn operator still provides a service no one can touch.

The Old Sale Barn

I wrote this poem about the old sale barn at Salida, Colorado. Though it's many owners, how the years have passed. The sale's now are seasonal but in the rush of the season, it continues to last. The sale barn was built in 1959. At that time it was owned by Carl Rundell and Loy Adams shortly after they opened Loy bought out Carl and for 5 or 6 years it was the largest sale barn in the state. In 1965 Loy sold the barn to Bill Davis. In 1968 Bill sold to Frits Rundell and the Hollbeck family. They continued to run it until health problems forced them to sell to Jack Jones and Gary Hill. It is currently owned by Larry Hughes. If only it could talk, what a story it would tell.

October 28, 1998

"The Old Sale Barn"

There is an old sale barn
On the east side of town
Its paint has all faded
And the pens are falling down

When the wind is blowing
You can hear the squeak of a hinge on a gate
I can remember in years past when trucks
Where in line and had to wait

If the old sale barn could talk
What a story it would tell
About the thousands of livestock sold
The different Auctioneers chants and the ringman's yell

It used to run day and night
And the pace ran without fail
They only stopped once in awhile
Just long enough to balance a scale

Now its days are numbered
And soon it will be torn down
Its use is no longer needed
And is being squeezed out by the growth of town

The Sale Barn Ghost

One night after the sale at Guymon, Oklahoma we came up short one cow. Everybody looked through all the pens and could not find her. The next morning I was in talking to the office manager Jeannie Cope when Butch Dickson stepped in and said, "Did the Sale Barn Ghost strike again?"

March 19, 2000

"The Sale Barn Ghost"

When they called me to the office
I knew something was really wrong
Things had been easy and smooth
All through the day long

It is a mystery that seems to happen
We do not know why or when
They said, "we are missing a cow"
It just happens now and then

Everybody has been out looking
We have checked every cow in the yards
She just seems to have disappeared
We have also checked all the dock cards

We hunted all day long
And even went back around the pens
All that I can come up with
The "Sale Barn Ghost" has struck again

My Market Philosophy

In 1996 I was helping an old family friend who was running the Sale Barn at Salida, Colorado the man was Richard Adams, a customer had brought his calves that day. The market may have been down, but I remember his words to this day.

September 1997

"My Market Philosophy"

Oh! Falls around the corner
And it's that time of year
Do I send my calves to the sale barn?
Or sell them at home here

I decide to sell at the sale barn
And I've called for a truck
One load of calves is all I have
And I hope to have good luck

When the markets down I have too many
And when it's up I have just a few
I know that the sale is not till Friday
And what they'll bring I wished I knew

Sale day comes around finally
And the market is down around here
They don't bring quite enough to pay the expenses
But shucks there's always next year

The Sorter

I wrote this poem when I was working for Bruce Gum at Guymon Livestock. It was raining and snowing when the sale was over, Bruce said to me, "what took you so long sorting?" It seems you took your time. I didn't have the nerve to tell him it was on his dime.

Thanks Bruce

Even though it was your dime, you left me with memories for my lifetime.

"The Sorter"

You start with a bunch of 100
And sort twenty ways
You just scratch your head
And say, "it's going to be one of those days"

You look for lumps, bumps and cripples
And you want the cattle to look right
You run your gate man ragged
From morning till night

But worst of all is getting kicked and ran over
Oh! You say it wouldn't happen if I wasn't slow
What really would help is if you
Would get this cow off of my toe

Cattle Buyer

Wow! This poem can cover a lot of ground. In my memory I have known so many cattle buyers, livestock dealers and traders just to name a few, Louis J. Head, Ward Sevier, Body Colbert, Dean Drake, Les Honey, Hank Wiescamp, Loy Adams, Orville Jones, Don Lane, Larry Wing, Buddy Waggoner, Jim Suckla, Billy Kahn, Pat Cugnini, Tex Vaughn, Coney Crain, Dan Colbert, Tex Vaughn, Dave Greenwalt, Merlin Williams and Zane Odell. I have to stop if I wrote all I know then I wouldn't have room for any more poems *Gentlemen this book is for you.*

April 16, 2000

"Cattle Buyer"

This man I'm going to tell about
Could be nicknamed aggravation
There seems to be one of his kind
Across this whole big nation

As he travels from farm to ranch
He doesn't really do any harm
But when he sees's something he likes
He can really put on the charm

When it comes to knowing cattle
He has an extra sharp eye
He's just trying to make a living
And wants his share of the pie

This man seems to be dedicated
His ambition never fades
It doesn't matter if it's 40 below
Or its hot and 110 in the shade

He may be a pain to the banker
Compared to a coyote he's a little slyer
A real problem to Vet's and Brand Inspectors
He's the local cattle buyer

Bad Day for the Boss

In January 2001, I was working for Bruce Gum at Guymon Livestock Auction, Guymo, Oklahoma. Bruce had sent me to Borger, Texas to represent the sale barn at a Jr. Livestock sale. Guess what, I got caught in a blizzard with no way to get home. Bruce called me and told me what was going on. I had to laugh because this is what happened to me every day. I worked for Bruce for several years and took care of the day to day problems. I have never regretted a minute that I worked for him.

January 11, 2001

"Bad Day for the Boss"

I was on the road the other day
When the boss gave me a call
By the sound of his voice
I was afraid he was going to bawl

He'd been up all night unloading trucks
Cause he couldn't get the night man out of bed
None of the help showed up that morning
And none of the cattle were fed

He had trucks come in all day
And he had cattle penned everywhere
By the tone of his voice
He was about to pull out his hair

He said he was just going home
He really didn't feel to well
The day things at the sale barn
Had just went plumb to Hell

The Trader

This is from memories when over forty years ago. As a kid I went to the local auction barn. They sold everything from household goods and livestock to stories. There was always a trader there. That bought anything. Now the old trader has faded away, but to me his memory will always stay.

March 27, 1999

"The Trader"

I was sitting in a sale the other day
When I noticed somebody that was gone
The old time trader has faded away
Times have made his living hard to get along

He's the one that went from sale to sale
And would buy anything from pigs, goats, to a cow
People came to him for the stories he would tell
He might never ever sell you a team and a plow

With his pickup and trailer he went around
Buying anything that would walk
He has a set of pens on the edge of town
And could sell you anything with his sales talk

But as times changes profits grew slim
It grew harder just to survive
Now its stories that remind us of him
It's up to writers like me to keep his memory alive

The Gambler

This poem goes with the cattle buyer and the trader. He was just a little more aggressive, spending money that was not his but hoping he'd make it before it was too late.

February 20, 1999

"The Gambler"

This man makes a living
Traveling from sale to sale
He order buys cattle
And always has a story to tell

In his daily trades in the country
He will get all he can on a truck
If he don't have a dead one
Then he thinks he's in luck

He may dream in bib overalls
Maybe even in a good suit
But if you don't watch him
You're the one that will pay the boot

He might drive a Cadillac
Or maybe an old beat up Ford
But it doesn't matter the crowd he's with
He will never act bored

His way of life is a gamble
On his trades from day to day
He just wants to make a living
Because he doesn't know another way

Rodeo

This is a place that I naturally got thrown into, when I was born. Before dad was a Brand Inspector, he was an auctioneer and rodeo announcer. I started out as a kid riding calves, then steers to bareback horses, team roping, calf roping and bull dogging. When I was 22 years old I got smart, why pay to have some fun when I could get paid to do it, so I started announcing rodeos. Well now 35 years later even though I have tried to quit someone talks me into doing one more. I have had the pleasure to announce rodeos in Colorado, New Mexico, Kansas, Nebraska, Texas, and Oklahoma. Oh how many fairs and small towns I've been to. I have no idea how many horse shows, team ropings, Jr. Livestock Shows, steer roping, or rodeo performances I have announced and I still enjoy it. I may say I want to quit, I can't there are too many friends still out there and I hope to meet more.

Cowboy Reunion

I have to say this is probably one of my favorite poems. After 20 some years of announcing rodeos, I started producing and announcing ranch rodeos in the southwest, Kansas, the Oklahoma and Texas panhandles. What a pleasure it was for me to do this. The cowboys were working cowboy's riding from daylight to dark, seven day's a week. I had a ranch rodeo at Guymon, Oklahoma and that evening all the wives were together and fixed supper, with forty teams entered there were over 300 people there. Yes we had sourdough, beef and beans. There were a couple guitars and a lot of singing. The next morning when I went to load the stock there were a lot of sleeping bags and tents scattered and horses hobbled everywhere. The wives fixed breakfast and everybody left. Even though they left in pickups and trailers, In my heart they are still what makes the west

October 3, 2000

"Cowboy Reunion"

They all drifted into camp
On a warm Saturday night
It took a lot of planning
Just to get things right

It was an old cowboy's reunion
They came from near and far
They were all carrying bedrolls
And a couple had brought a guitar

With supper around the chuck wagon
The usual fare of sourdough, beef and beans
Cooked on a campfire in Dutch ovens
Not a one left hungry by any means

They sat on their bedrolls
And the stories they could tell
About all the bronc's they rode
And cattle along the trail

They all remembered in silence
In the camp there wasn't a dry eye
About all their old partners
That drifted to the big ranch in the sky

In the morning each was up early
They saddled and went separate ways
There was not a good bye said
They knew they'd see each other one of these days

Just to be there to see it
What a sight it was to me
The old cowboy's from the past
From the old days we'll never get to see

Mr. Rodeo

I could write all day and still not tell about all the good things Edker Wilson has done. This poem relates to the poem of friends, I just wanted to thank Edker for being such a good friend and influence on me.

March 15, 1999

"Mr. Rodeo"

When the announcer introduces him
Across the speakers clear and loud
He humbly steps in front of the chutes
And waves his hat to salute the crowd

From the Utah and Colorado mountains
To the desert's of Arizona and New Mexico
He is loved and known by many
When he puts on their hometown rodeo

Bulls and bronc's have been his living
For almost fifty years in the west
Putting on good rodeo's everywhere
Is what he is known for best

From a champion to a beginner
He wishes them all good luck
He calls everyone of them son
And is glad to lend them an extra buck

He travels fifty-two weeks a year
Putting on Rodeo's is his game
From small towns to big cities
And Edker Wilson is his name

Rodeo Time

Since I was a kid and through the years I have been a contestant and also have announced rodeos for 35 years. There is not a time that I don't think about Edker Wilson, this is about him. He called all of the boys son and called the girls hon. Edker is now some 90 years young and still going strong.

May 26, 2007

"Rodeo Time"

Oh it happens every year this time
You are ready to leave home
In your pocket you have a dime
Just to make a call on the phone

For the next few weeks you go
There's not a horse that bucks hard
Or a steer that runs slow
But that man still calls you pard

Now it is the middle of July
You sit on your rigging bag
And just ask yourself why
You tried hard and didn't brag

But if you think what is wrong
And there is no one there for you
Just drop your quarter in the jukebox
That will always make it through

Though you look towards the fall
And you try, ride and rope hard
You know you will conquer all
Just remember the man called you pard

Then when the season ends
And the championships you won
Always remember Edker Wilson
He's the one that called you son

Mr. Bronc Man

I was watching RFD TV one day and the show Rodeo Behind the Chutes when they interviewed Mr. Vold. Anyone that's been involved in rodeo knows of Harry Vold. He has probably owned more great bucking horses than anyone in the PRCA and has produced some of the largest Rodeos in the United States, I have had the pleasure to meet and talk to Harry many times through the years.
I would like to include in this the Etbauer brothers, Billy, Robert and Dan and mention that I've had the pleasure of being good friends with Robert and Dan

May 26, 2007.

"Mr. Bronc Man"

When I think of this man
He will never brag and boast
But when it comes to him
I will stand and make a toast

Bronc riders I have known
Through so many years
When your horses bucked them off
I saw their wives in tears

These three brothers never brag
Bout themselves but always had a plan
That was Robert, Billy and Dan

These men were all bronc riders
They never thought they were great
But when they were mounted
They weren't afraid to nod for the gate

But you bucked them off many times
And you and your horses were never bold
You are the one I respect and probably the best
My hats off to you Mr. Harry Vold

Out of Chew

Well this is for anybody that Rodeo's and chews, you gamble on winning. This did really happen to a friend of mine Tommy Meyers and myself when we were in high school in Salida, Colorado.

December 25, 1998

"Out of Chew"

It's the Fourth of July roping
And were headed for the dough
Cause we rope might fast
And the other teams are slow

Tom settles in the box and nods
And ropes the head real neat
I come in on the corner
And plumb miss both hind feet

Now were leaving and heading home
And we don't really know what to do
We'll have to get a real job tomorrow
Were not only out of beer money,

Now were out of chew

Stranger

In 2002 I was very fortunate to announce steer ropin's for the Invitational Steer Roping Association. The finals that year were at Amarillo, Texas. Due to association rule's any cowboy that was in the top 20 steer roping in the PRCA couldn't compete. Buster Record of Buffalo, Oklahoma and the current world champion were there as field judges. When the stories circulated around about how Buster had started out. I will admit this poem is probably not 100 percent accurate. I just wanted to make a point.

February 19, 2002

"Stranger"

We all noticed and watched him
As he rode around the grounds
We had never seen him before
He was a stranger in town

He was riding a big buckskin horse
And his rigging was patched up tack
His boots were scuffed and a hole in his hat
There were holes in the shirt on his back

He went to the office to enter
As he passed he never cracked a smile
He entered the steer roping
Said he hadn't roped for awhile

He laid down his first steer
And tied three feet fast
He tied his next two steers
We knew our chances wouldn't last

When it was over he loaded up and left
We heard about him later that fall
He was the World Champion Steer Roper
The stranger that beat us all

The Coffee Shop Cowboy's

Now every true cowboy knows that the worst thing to have around is a team roper. But when you have two of them things are going to hell. This poem is dedicated to these team ropers. My brother Jim Bertrand, Stan Embry, Don Pease, Denzil Goodwin, Gene Bondurant, Tim & Dale Meyers, Don Porco, and Jerry Dominic

Sorry guys' paybacks are hell

"The Coffee Shop Cowboys"

They get up early in the morning
And head to the café
It's just out of habit
But it's the way they start their day

They've rode bulls and broncs in Canada
Roped in Denver for thousands or so
They have done it all
Even roped for a few bucks in El Paso

Every one of them has been
To every rodeo and roping to ride
From north and south to east and west
And even over the Great Divide

Their talk is low and humble
They don't ever yell
They just gather round their table
Cause they all have a windy to tell

Rodeo Cowboys and Gates

When I started to work for Bruce Gum at Guymon livestock, Bruce told me about what happened the first week of May. When the Guymon Pioneer Day's was going on. He donated the use of the pens at the sale barn for the timed events for the cowgirls and cowboys, I started to work for Bruce in 1996 three years later this poem came to mind. We were taking delivery of about 3000 head of futures cattle plus a sale of around 400 head, when I got there at four in the morning. There wasn't a cowboy there. But where there horses were, every gate was open.

May 4, 1999

"Rodeo Cowboy's and Gates

Well I wanted to tell a story
About good old traveling lads
It's just hard to believe
They never listened to their dads

They travel from rodeo to rodeo
And they are the best
From roping to dogging
They're winners across the west

But here at Guymon Livestock
They come the first weekend in May
The cowboy's really try hard
To stay out of the way

They can rope a steer or calf
With speed and grace under eight
But one thing they can't do
They can't learn to shut a gate

When a Legend Fades

I wrote this poem about Buddy Heaton of Hugohton, Kansas. Yes, Buddy did some crazy things and was notorious for things he had done. But one thing I can say, he was always a honest wit

September 1998

"When a Legend Fades"

The other day on a lonesome Kansas highway
A man was walking alone
I slowed down and stopped
And gave him a ride home

When he got in the pick-up
It didn't take long for me to recognize
That here was a legend—
From rodeo days that have gone by

He was one of the best
And had been on top of that golden dome
Also that the trip back down
Had been made by him alone

The friends he had made were many
Such as a hero in any sport will do
But his memory has faded
And his friends number just a few

It was in front of his house
That I saw the glimmer of a tear in his eye
I knew then that he sat in hopes
That an old friend would come by

Windmills

When I was a field rep for Bruce Gum and Guymon Livestock, my travels took me from northeastern New Mexico, southern Colorado, southwestern Kansas, and the panhandles of Oklahoma and Texas. I saw first hand how the rancher depended on their windmills, they always took time to work on them when needed. The days and hours they spent working on them preserved their livelihood.

January 4, 1999

"Wind Mills"

There on top of the flat
Stands an old wooden windmill
That has done its work for years
And has always had water to spill

Many horses and cows
Have come to the tank
Spent the day grazing
And at morning and night they drank

The old wooden blades still turn
As the wind constantly blows
How many head have watered there
No one really knows

That old windmill still does its duty
Come wind, rain or shine
Through drought and hardships
It's pumped water that is fine

To the rancher that owns it
It has earned its place
And he works on it when needed
So it never had to be replaced

"Nature"

These poems are about the way that nature has its own way of making things balance out. I believe the best way to get along with nature is not to fight it, but let things take their course. Since we have no control anyway. So the right thing to do is make the best of any situation.

Weather Changes

Not much to say here, just a poem I wrote about the weather and how it affects us all.

December 20, 1998

"Weather Changes"

I remember growing up in the mountains
And thought we had bad snow
Until I moved on the plains
And lived through a blow

It started out as what I thought was a skift
Coming down hard and sideways
And then it began to drift
Lasting for several days

Riding in a valley in a mountain drizzle
On the plains it comes down hard
With a violent thunder making your hair frizzle
Causing water to bounce across the yard

In the mountains the marble size hail is soft
But on the plains it's the size of golf balls
Knocking out a barn loft
And tearing down the walls

Or sitting around a campfire
In a cool evening breeze
While on the plains the wind
Will bring you to your knees

No Rain

This poem can probably be one that anyone anywhere can relate to.
Because drought can hit anywhere any time. Now I live in the southwestern
corner of Colorado, I call this the land of the five too's, it is either too hot,
too dry, too cold or too wet.
I'd leave here but I'm too damn broke.

December 20, 1999

"No Rain"

There's nowhere worse to live
Than in cow country with no rain
The ranchers act real funny
You start to think they're insane

They get grouchy with their wives
And cuss and holler at their dogs
They start having daydreams
Of pulling cows out of a bog

He cusses the weatherman and bankers
And the feed salesmen are everywhere
He knows he will need the feed
But they're like buzzards in the air

The drought causes the grass to shrivel
And the cows to get real thin
He has real bad nightmares
Of having to haul water again

All of a sudden it starts raining
For days it comes with a big roar
He starts out across the country
And hopes it doesn't rain anymore

"My Horses"

I've had horses of every kind
But there are several
Those always come to mind
With all types of colors

From palominos, buckskins and grays
Sooner I brought one home
To paints, appys and bays
To a one eyed blue roan

I've rode all kinds
From broke horses to colts and a mule
But thee was one sorrel gelding
Those always made me look like a fool

But I always remember
Through the work, crashes, or a fall
There wasn't any great ones
But each was best of all

The Trainer

This is about probably what I would call my glory years. When I was in high school, I worked for Dr. V.A. Veltri. Doc had three horse trainers. Though I mainly cleaned stalls and ponied horses. I will always remember these three Bill Atchison, Bill Anderson, and Gene Teffertiller.

January 1, 1998

"The Trainer"

He comes out of the tack room
With an arm load of tack
It's a might hard living
Being a trainer on the track

He starts early and feeds them all
Each horse is watered and groomed
And starts to clean each stall
It's a daily chore that has to be done

He saddles his pony horse at eight
And takes some to gallop
He needs to break one to the starting gate
And has four cooling on the walker

On race day he just wants a good race
He wants the starter to be fair at the gate
To break the horses even and in line
And make sure one doesn't start late

And after the winners circle he wants to test clean
Because winning the All American Futurity
Has been his lifetime dream
And he knows he has done the best he can

The Last of the Wild Ones

No, this is not about the BLM horses but about a bunch of wild horses I had the pleasure to see. In central Colorado in the late 1920's and 30's horses weren't worth much. In that time south of Hartsell, Colorado to Canon City there was a band of scrub mares that had been abandoned and neglected from the people that moved to Colorado Springs and Pueblo. A few of the South Park Rangers turned out a few thoroughbred studs to these mares. I had the pleasure to own one of the last colts of this band, he was mean, about half crazy, yet one of the best horses I ever had.

January 10, 1999

"The Last of the Wild Ones"

When I first saw him he turned and fled
His bulging muscles glistening in the sun
Up and over the rim rock he sped
It was amazing how fast he could run

He nickered and gathered his broodmare band
They all moved out at breakneck speed
The mighty wild horse of the desert land
A rainbow of colors of an unknown breed

For years they have been chased and caught
To be gathered, broke and sold
They learned to live with man as taught
But some remain wild until they're old

But to me their years of being alive
In this arid harsh and bitter land
Through hardships they endure and survive
Their biggest problem is urban growth
created by man

"The Renegade Mules"

Ol' Tom and I were grinning like fools
We decided today was the day
We were gonna catch the renegade mules

We mount our horses and build our loops
Tom runs upon one and ropes his neck
I catch both hind feet with one scoop

Tom jumps off to tie him down
As he gets to him
My horse gives some slack
If you coulda see it ol' Tom looked like a clown

The mule was braying, pawing and things like that
Ol' Tom came up grinning and said this is like
When I put super glue in my hand to catch a bobcat

On that day it's needless to say
With the beating and pawing he took
Tom was glad that mule got away

January 4, 1999

Yard Sale Queens

To an auctioneer yard sales are a nightmare. When you go to one and basically see things being given away. In any city, town or community on any given weekend these gals loose complete control and go to everyone. I don't begrudge them getting bargains I do it myself. But here's to you girls "The Yard Sale Queens"

March 6, 2009

"Yard Sale Queens"

They are an auctioneer's nightmare
In search of anything they can find
If they come to an auction
They won't even bid a dime

But when it comes to a yard sale
They travel like flocks of geese
Across the lawn's and tables
They pillar and they fleece

Looking for bargains that are cheap
From clothes to dishes, even books
If you beat em to a treasure
You sure can get some dirty looks

Now across this great nation
In every city and town it seems
On any weekend they hunt and search
They are the mighty Yard Sale Queens

"American Farmer"

In his mind there was a dream
On a hill out on the plains
All he had was a wagon and team
He hoped that there was rain

With his family on a homestead
Talking care of crops day to day
He kept his family clothed and fed
Working hard he knew it was there way

As the years of work went by
And his small family grew
Living by his work ethics
They each knew what to do

And now three generations have held on
Raising cattle, corn and wheat
With high taxes and expenses all along
They still produce grain and meat

Americans need to honor this kind of man
Across the country from east to west
It was men like him across this great land
That made this Nation the best

June 4, 2004

The Local Politician

I wrote this poem about a friend of my families. I was living at Nathrop, Colorado at the time. Frank McMurray was running for county commissioner. On Saturdays a bunch of us would meet at the Centerville Pit Stop for coffee. On Saturday morning about 10:30 I was the only one at the store when Frank came in to get coffee, he had a stunned look and said to me, "where is everybody? I was going to buy the coffee."

October 1996

"The Local Politician"

It's six am and he jumps up with a smile
He's a local politician
And for the voter, he'll drive the extra mile
It's to the radio station

To the local forum, you see
For debates with opponents
Just for you and me
Then to the newspaper office

He has to because of the need
He looks up the statistics
To see if he is in the lead
It's off to the coffee shop

He walks in and sits at a table
All crowded with a bunch
He says "Dang, I'm too late to buy coffee
And too early to buy lunch

Make It Beef

This is another poem that just happened. While I was at Guymon Livestock, Juanita Gray was managing the restaurant and for her special on sale day, she had chicken and noodles. Bruce Gum the barn's owner got mad and said to Nita, he didn't give a Damn what she fixed, but we were in the cattle business and from then on it had better be beef. I was very fortunate after I wrote this poem that the Oklahoma Beef Council used it.

March 27, 1999

"Make It Beef"

When its time to fix something to eat
And you don't know really what is good
When you go to the store for some meat
Please make mine beef if you would

Now fish is a good change sometimes
And can be tasty now and then
Chicken and Pork will work in a bind
But I'd prefer beef again

There's nothing better than a good steak
With potato and trimmings on the side
But if you're not real hungry and need a break
Try one with a salad that makes it light

You can bake, slice, grind and fry it
From China, Italian, Swiss and a Mexican dish
Or do like the Texans and cook it in a pit
It doesn't matter the cut its what you wish

You may live in a city penthouse
Or on a big coastal reef
But when your're cooking a meal
Always remember to try *beef*

The Week before Christmas

Though it's sad to say when I first wrote this poem, I had just started to write poems. This still remains to me one of the worst ones I have written, though at the same time Outta the Chute Rodeo Publications which at that time was the official rodeo paper for several rodeo associations. They picked this poem for *Poem of the Year*. Duh what do I know?

December 20, 1996

"The Week before Christmas"

Twas a week before Christmas
And all was well
It was down at the sale barn
That things went to hell

Old Santa had flew in
Just on a test flight
He knew right away
He would never make things right

Old John Ward or the boys
Never looked or cared
About his sleighful of toys
They just looked around and dared

Who could buy his reindeer, harness and sleigh
How long would it take to loose
All of the profit in yardage and hay
Or where they could sell them and make the news

They knew right away they needed some luck
Because Santa stepped and what he said
Made their tails tuck
And even made them bow their head

Old Santa said to the traders you see
Christmas aint for profit or greed
We try to help others
And people in need

So you have a Merry Christmas
And a Happy New Year
And the goat I just sold you
Is really not a miniature reindeer

"Christmas Eve"

Twas the night before Christmas
I know it will be hard to believe
But this is what happened to me
On this years Christmas Eve

My buddy and I were at cow camp
He was sitting telling a yarn
I was just listening to him
When I heard noises to the barn

I took out hurrying to the barn
Inside there was Santa and his sleigh
He and his reindeer were shook up
They were dirty and covered with hay

He said while flying over a mountain
They clipped a tree, he was sure smug
They were travelin at break neck speed
And broke a runner and snapped a tug

We went to the tack room for repairs
With bailing wire, leather and twine
We worked fast splicing everything together
Santa looked and said that was fine

Santa said he needs to leave
They took off with little noise
He had a hard night ahead
Delivering presents to little girls and boys

As I stood waved and watched them leave
I looked around and had to smile
I didn't know if I was dreaming
But I know it was all worthwhile

December 20, 2007

New Years Eve

Last New Years, my daughter Dusti asked me to watch the kids. Even though they are well mannered and quiet they still put me to the test. But you guessed it as a grandpa I always enjoy being with them.

"New Years Eve"

I was just sitting at home
It is really hard to explain
I've been through blizzards and tornados
But this was worse than hail or rain

It was on New Years Eve
And all was well and quiet
When Dusti and Casey dropped off the kids
The monsters, Hailey, Kendra and Wyatt"

Now they are great kids
And I love them all the same
But when they start crying
I can't remember their names

Now its late and past midnight
And I don't really know what to do
The kids are all crying
And Hailey says Grandpa I love you

My daughter Dusti is very special
And I love her don't you see
I just hope she hurries back
To get these monsters off of me

Now I do know in the morning
They will come dragging along
Lord I just pray and hope
They take these kids were they belong

Now they went with their mom and dad
To the house they call home
And everything is good and well
Now I can let the dog out to roam

I do love these grandkids
And I hope it aint too late
But if their mom calls again
I am going out on a date

"Christmas"

Have you noticed the peace and quiet
Once a year on a certain morn
When on that day around the world
We celebrate when Christ was born

When early on Christmas morning
As you feed and harness the team
Everything is quiet and peaceable
And the stars have a different gleam

The teams feet beet a rhythmic pace
As you cut the hay strings with a knife
To feed the cattle for the day
The still morning makes you appreciate life

When you head back to the house and barns
The team begins to pick up speed
They seem to know that on this day
They will get extra care and feed

Later the family will gather round the tree
Open presents, enjoy a meal and to play
To wish all a Merry Christmas
And celebrate this special birthday!

December 17, 1999

"Christmas Alone"

Well the time is near
And it's Christmas Eve
And not to long, till a new year

Once again everyone is at home
There's a customer at the dock, one in the office
And danged if there isn't three on the phone

I'm trying to feed some hay
But everything's going wrong
And it's starting to be a long day

I have so much to do; I don't know where to start
But with everyone else gone
I'm trying to keep it from coming apart

I hope by dark I get home
Because there's nothing worse on Christmas
Than being stuck at the sale barn alone

December 24, 1998

Angels of Love

A person may never think about a nurse or how important their job is.
About the stress and many hours they put in. I wrote this for all nurses everywhere. In Guymon I had been injured and had gangrene and a staph infection. With six and a half days in the hospital I saw how important they were.
I dedicate this to all nurses everywhere.

May 26, 2007

"Angles of Love"

I want to start this about a well known tale
About a loving and caring lady of the past
Through history known as Miss Nightingale

The same dedicated lady is still here
She will always be there for you
Through you and you're family fears

The hours of sacrifice she has done
To be there care and comfort you
She tries hard to help everyone

She's there always, when you're in need
Always taking care of your loved ones
Because in her heart she made a deed

Her workday is very hard and long
The doctor tells her what to do
She doesn't argue and say it is wrong

Through her life she's given up so much
Herself in life and family have suffered
Just to give a patient a caring touch

But before you gripe and complain
Remember this special lady was there
To help you through suffering and pain

When everything is right and you smile
Just remember this special angel
In her mind and heart it was all worthwhile

Edwards Brothers Malloy
Thorofare, NJ USA
March 5, 2014